The Opinements of Regis and Angus:
The World View
of Two
Scottish Terriers

Written and Illustrated by:

Lauren McKune

AuthorHouse™
1663 Liberty Drive
Bloomington, IN 47403
www.authorhouse.com
Phone: 833-262-8899

Because of the dynamic nature of the Internet, any web addresses or links contained in this book may have changed since publication and may no longer be valid. The views expressed in this work are solely those of the author and do not necessarily reflect the views of the publisher, and the publisher hereby disclaims any responsibility for them.

Any people depicted in stock imagery provided by Getty Images are models, and such images are being used for illustrative purposes only.
Certain stock imagery © Getty Images.

This book is printed on acid-free paper.

ISBN: 978-1-4389-2830-2 (sc)

Library of Congress Control Number: 2008909856

Print information available on the last page.

Published by AuthorHouse 02/03/2021

authorHOUSE®

This book is dedicated to everyone who loves to laugh, and especially those who laugh, as a means to love.

Pedestrians. That sounds so regal. Must be the king's english?

Yeah, they definitely mean you and me. Or is it you and I?

REGIS AND ANGUS   BY LAUREN MCKUNE

Angus, doesn't this vast body of water remind you of Lake Lochness?

Oh yes Regis! And look, they have a monster too!

Hey Angus, have you ever noticed how bagpipes have much in common with politicians?

Yes Regis, both can be full of hot air and most annoying.

REGIS AND ANGUS   BY LAUREN MCKUNE

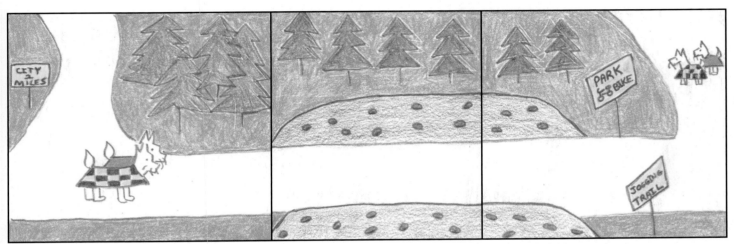

Angus, we are very brave lads to be walking through this forest.

Yes Regis, there's no telling what danger lurks ahead.

REGIS AND ANGUS   BY LAUREN MCKUNE

Regis, are you thinking what I'm thinking?

Well Angus, to paraphrase Roy Orbison ♪ whoa, whoa pretty lassie. ♪

6

Regis, I love golf courses because of the beautiful greens, and of course, they remind me of home. So why do you love golf courses?

Angus, I have a compulsion for argyle socks. But don't worry, I'm working on it.

Regis, why do Americans love fast food?

Why do you think I love argyle socks, Angus? I just have to have them.

REGIS AND ANGUS   BY LAUREN MCKUNE

Regis, I have my deepest and most profound thoughts during times of inclement weather. How about you?

Does wishing for an umbrella count?

Regis, I am learning so much about geneology.

Do you ever wonder about your ancestral roots? Or perhaps, where your name originated?

Well Angus, rumor has it a gentleman, named Regis, has a talk show in New York. Maybe he's a distant cousin?

Do you believe in Santa Claus Regis?

Why do you think I hang up red and green argyles every year?

Regis, isn't the harbor's
fireworks display wonderful?

Regis? Hey... Regis?

I cannot believe you're
wearing ear muffs,
lad. That's just
embarrassing.

Hey Regis, that lassie looks very familiar to me.

Let's just say Angus, like you, she has a definite style.

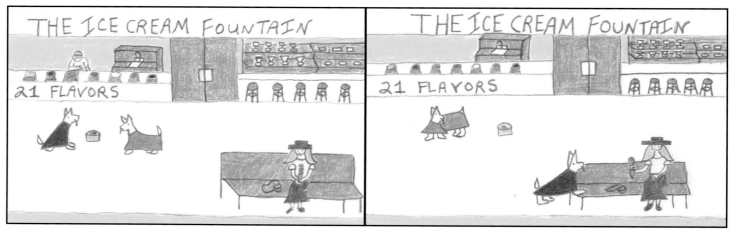

Regis, wasn't it lucky to get an ice cream sample? I cannot think of anything better.

I can Angus. Does the word "trifecta," mean anything to you, lad?

Angus, it was a splendid idea of yours to visit the arboretum. The plants and trees are so exquisite.

And speaking of things exquisite, look at the beautiful peacock, Regis. She is exceptional.

Angus, I hate to spoil your enthusiasm, but all ornate peacocks are male identified.

In that case, Regis, let's just say he's a regal looking lad.

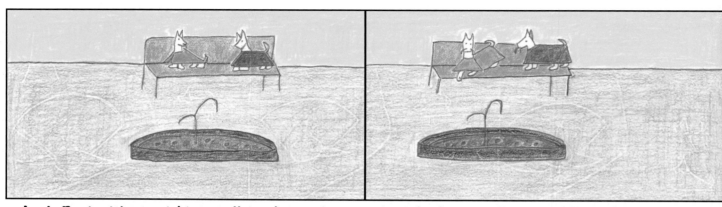

Look Regis, it's a wishing well in the park. Now let's see. Ah yes, I wish that you and I remain friends, until the sun ceases to shine. How about you Regis?

I wish that I will always have frequent encounters with argyle socks. Preferably, gold and blue colored. Oh, and Angus, I will be your friend, even after, the sun ceases to shine.

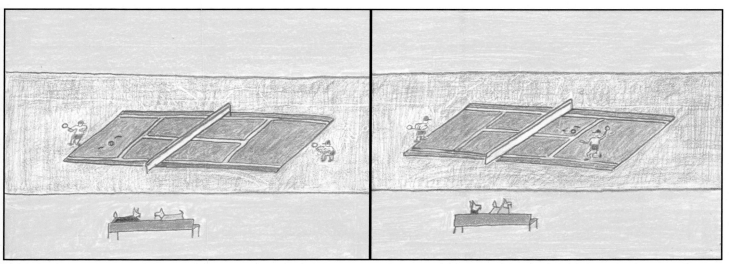

Don't you enjoy watching a competitive game of tennis, Regis?

Not nearly, as much as, I enjoy watching the white argyles worn by the players, lad.

Oh Regis, doesn't visiting the zoo remind you of the film "Out of Africa?"

Well, actually Angus, visiting the zoo is a little more of a challenge for me, lad.

How so Regis?

Well, rather than "Out of Africa," I am reminded of the films "Top Gun" and "Rin, Tin, Tin." In short lad, I feel like I'm in the "danger zone" and my mind keeps telling me run, Regis, run!

REGIS AND ANGUS   BY LAUREN MCKUNE

Hey Regis, look at the baby ducklings.

I don't believe I have seen anything more adorable.

Well Angus, if you and I were wearing our sportive tartans, we could definitely come in a close second, lad.

Regis, what's the difference between a Democrat and a Republican politician?

About the same difference between a coke and a pepsi, lad.

Hey look Regis, our friend Sam is wanted. Do you think we should phone and let them know he's on vacation?

Angus, let's just drop off the postcard he sent from Catalina, inside his owner's mailbox.

Now, that's think'in like a Lincoln, lad.

REGIS AND ANGUS   BY LAUREN MCKUNE

Regis, why is the cost of fuel so high?

Angus do you remember Hans Christian Andersen's "The Emperor's New Clothes"?

Yes lad, I do.

Well, like the characters in that children's story, people are too afraid to state the obvious.

Oh my! You mean President Bush walks around in the nude, lad?

Certainly not, Angus. But like the emperor, his poorer judgement has become, most transparent.

Now let's find us some tea.

REGIS AND ANGUS   BY LAUREN MCKUNE

Regis, I so enjoy nature. I've been wondering if you might explain global warming to me, lad.

Ah yes, global warming. Well Angus, it is a phenomenon whereby, industrial emissions create greenhouse gases. And of course, the United States declined to ratify the Kyoto agreement.

And why was that Regis?

Well, the Bush administration failed to understand that ignorance can be, as dangerous as, a whole in the ozone layer.

So is meandering in the street, Regis.

Let's move to the sidewalk, lad.

Oh how I love the tradition of Halloween, Regis. I'm so excited about trick or treating. I can't wait to arrive at the front door in our colorful tartans.

My goodness Regis, look at all the candy we received. I told you the lady of the house would be impressed with our festive dress.

Angus, dear friend, I think she was a little more taken with my "sleight of hand." Did you see how her eyes widened and her mouth opened, after I left with her husband's orange argyles?

You're right Regis. That was an impressive trick, lad.

REGIS AND ANGUS   BY LAUREN MCKUNE

Oh Regis, I do admire those who are bold and adventurous enough to ride a hot air balloon. What do you think, lad?

Quite frankly Angus, aside from the awesome view, riding a hot air balloon is not as compelling as riding on a congested freeway. With fuel costing on average $4.50 a gallon, now that can be a bold adventure friend.

Touché Regis, touché.

Now remember Angus, you are not a strong swimmer. I don't want you embarrassing us with Ms. Sophie over there.

Oh stop worrying Regis. I can always dog paddle, lad.

REGIS AND ANGUS   BY LAUREN MCKUNE

Going to the amusement park is such fun Regis. I especially love the challenge of riding the roller coaster. Oh, by the way, I want to thank you for accompanying me Regis. I know how you despair of heights.

Angus, if I can just manage walking a straight line, after we ride this coaster, I will have dodged the moniker "stupidity in motion," and hopefully, saved a little dignity for myself lad.

So, I guess that means we will be skipping the parachute ride then, Regis?

REGIS AND ANGUS   BY LAUREN MCKUNE

Regis, since the American election is in November, I've been wondering what qualities, you think, make for a good president.

Well lad, a president must possess a fine intellect, moral integrity, a sense of humor, and finally, a charisma that resonates with the populace.

Gosh Regis, you just described Abraham Lincoln.

Yes lad, I believe I did.

By the way Angus, Lincoln is the "gold standard" by which all presidents are judged.

So Regis, how do you think history will define the Bush administration?

As the "substandard" presidency, lad.

And by that Regis, you mean?

I mean Angus, his dog Barney, could have done a better job!

REGIS AND ANGUS   BY LAUREN MCKUNE

Are you sure you don't want to skate Regis? There's no need to be afraid of the ice, lad.

Afraid? Of course not Angus! I'm just trying to visualize my moves before I make them.

For example, the "Regis free fall." That's when I take to the ice, trip over my ice skates and slide, ever so gracefully, across the rink.

And with that being said, Regis, I give you a perfect "10" for creative avoidance.

REGIS AND ANGUS   BY LAUREN MCKUNE

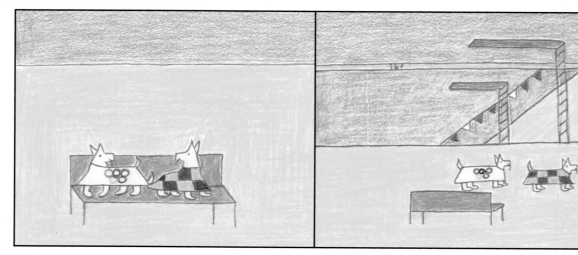

Regis, I'm so excited about the 2008 Olympics in Beijing, that I purchased a commemorative sweater. Isn't it colorful?

Yes Angus, but do you know the flag's history, lad?

Actually, no Regis, I don't.

Well Angus, the five rings and colors are representative of those continents participating in the games.

Also, the flag's colors: blue, black, red, yellow and green each represent at least one of the colors found in a participant's national flag.

And finally, the overall purpose of the Olympics, Angus, is to join the world together, in the name of sports.

Boy Regis, you sure are profound. In fact, you're deeper than an Olympic size pool. You're even deeper than...

Okay Angus, I get the point.

REGIS AND ANGUS   BY LAUREN MCKUNE

Regis, who do you think will be elected president in November, Senator McCain or Senator Obama?

Quite frankly Angus, you just might want to consult a higher authority.

Certainly you're not suggesting God?

Oh Angus, of course not! I'm referring to the U.S. Supreme Court.

But Regis, the justices represent the judiciary branch of power. They're not to decide such things.

I know, lad!

Are you chidding me Regis?

No Angus, however, I may be chadding you.

31

Printed in the United States
By Bookmasters